ANIMALS UNDER T~~~
GREAT WHITE SHARK

IN DANGER OF EXTINCTION!

Richard Spilsbury

Heinemann Library
Chicago, Illinois

Designed by Jo Hinton-Malivoire and Tokay,
   Bicester, UK (www.tokay.co.uk)
Picture Research by Rosie Garai and Liz Eddison
Originated by Ambassador Litho Ltd.
Printed in China by WKT
Company Limited

08 07 06 05 04
10 9 8 7 6 5 4 3 2 1

**Library of Congress Cataloging-in-Publication
Data**
Spilsbury, Richard.
   Great white shark / Richard Spilsbury.
      p. cm. -- (Animals under threat)
Summary: Discusses the plight of great white
sharks and why they are near extinction, as well
as some of the ways humans can help.
Includes bibliographical references and index.
   ISBN 1-4034-4860-4 (lib. bdg.) -- ISBN 1-4034-
5434-5 (pbk.)
   1. White shark--Juvenile literature. [1. White
sharks. 2. Sharks. 3. Endangered species.] I.
Spilsbury, Richard, 1963- II. Title. III.
Series.
QL638.95.L3S56 2004
597.3'3--dc22
                                        2003016140

Acknowledgments
The author and publishers are grateful to the
following for permission to reproduce copyright
material:
p. 4 David Fleetham/Oxford Scientific Films; p. 5
Pacific Stock/Bruce Coleman; pp. 6, 10, 25, 28, 22
Ron and Valerie Taylor/Ardea; p. 8 Mark
Bowler/NHPA; p. 9 National Geographic/Brian
Skerry/Getty Images; p. 11 Jim Watt/Bruce
Coleman; p. 12 Valerie Taylor/Ardea; p. 13 Stuart
Westmorland/Corbis; pp. 14, 15, 18, 41 Ralf
Kiefner/Ardea; p. 16 Tom Heald/Nature Picture
Library; p. 19 Rex/Greg Williams; pp. 20, 24, 35
Corbis; p. 21 Nature Picture Library; p. 23
Inc/Villoch-Visual&Witte/Bruce Coleman; pp. 26,
32, 39 Jeffrey L. Rotman/Corbis; p. 27 Norbert
Wu/NHPA; p. 29 Trevor McDonald/NHPA; p. 30
Tobians Bernhard/Oxford Scientific Films; p. 31
Howard Hall/Oxford Scientific Films; p. 33 ANT
Photolibrary/NHPA; p. 34 Peter Steyn/Ardea; pp.
36, 37 EPA/PA; p. 38 Jeff Rotman/Getty Images; p.
42Plymouth Aquarium; p. 43 Tudor Photography.

Cover photograph reproduced with permission of
Bruce Coleman/Jim Watt.

Every effort has been made to contact copyright
holders of any material reproduced in this book.
Any omissions will be rectified in subsequent
printings if notice is given to the publisher.

Disclaimer
All the Internet addresses (URLs) given in this
book were valid at the time of going to press.
However, due to the dynamic nature of the
Internet, some addresses may have changed, or
sites may have ceased to exist since publication.
While the author and publisher regret any
inconvenience this may cause readers, no
responsibility for any such changes can be
accepted by either the author or the publisher.

The paper used to print this book comes from
sustainable resources.

Some words are shown in bold, **like
this.** You can find out what they mean
by looking in the glossary.

Contents

The Great White Shark

Sharks are fish

All fish are **vertebrates** that live in water. Most fish swim using fins. They breathe through **gills**, their skins are covered in **scales** and they produce soft eggs. Scientists organize fish into three groups based on their skeletons: **bony fish** have hard, bony skeletons; **cartilaginous fish** have softer skeletons; and jawless fish have no jawbones. Sharks, and their close relatives the skates and rays, are types of cartilaginous fish.

The great white shark has a bad reputation. People think it will kill almost anything in the water, including them. In fact, these remarkable creatures are not very well understood. A great white shark is quite picky about what it eats, and it lives a secretive life. It is also an **endangered species.** This means there are so few of them left in the oceans that they are at risk of becoming **extinct.** There is only one reason for this: people kill great whites at a faster rate than the sharks can have young, so their numbers drop.

This book is about the life of great white sharks, and why and how people kill them. It also looks at the efforts being made by some people to protect this shark and to save it from extinction.

▲ *The great white shark* (Carcharodon carcharias) *is an awesome* **predator.**

▲ *The biggest great white sharks can weigh over 3 tons.*

The sharks

The great white is one of around 400 different species of shark. Sharks vary greatly in shape, from T-shaped hammerheads to frilly wobbegongs. They also come in many sizes, from 6-inch-long (16-centimeter-long) lanternsharks to 39-foot-long (12-meter-long) whale sharks. The great white belongs to the mackerel shark family.

Mackerel sharks all have a body shaped like a torpedo with a large tail **fin** shaped like a crescent moon. This is joined to the rest of their body by a narrow tail stalk. They have one large triangular **dorsal** fin and a second tiny dorsal fin nearer their tail. Their ten **gill slits**—five on each side—are long and wrap around the sides of their body. Mackerel sharks also have a pointed snout and large, dark eyes.

Adult great whites are the largest flesh-eating sharks. The only two larger species of shark in the world, the whale shark and the basking shark, both feed on tiny animals in the water. Great whites can grow to more than 19 feet (6 meters) long, but are usually closer to 13 feet (4 meters). Females are generally bigger than males, but they look very similar.

Why "great white?"

Great whites are not completely white. Although they have a white belly and sides, they have a darker back in a shade of grey or olive. There are no white sharks. Most people call them "great" whites because of their size and power. Some other names for the great white include white pointer, man-eater, jaws, and white death!

Where Do Great White Sharks Live?

Nearly all **species** of shark spend their whole lives in seawater. Most kinds of shark live only in **tropical** waters. Here the water remains at a similar warm temperature all year around. However, great white sharks live mostly in cooler waters between 55 °F and 68 °F (13 °C and 20 °C). These cooler waters are where most of their **prey** lives.

Great whites live in and move between oceans all around the world. But there are more of them in the waters around southern Africa from Namibia to South Africa, southern Australia, Japan, northeastern and southwestern United States, and in the southern Mediterranean. Individual sharks sometimes stick around favorite areas. In one Australian population, about one third of the sharks stayed around the same place throughout the year.

The right temperature

Sharks, like all fish, are **cold-blooded.** This means that the temperature of their bodies is usually the same as the water around them. Different sharks have adapted to live at different temperatures. If a tropical shark is put into cold water, it slows down because there is not enough warmth for it to remain active. Water temperature is affected not only by **climate** and season, but also by water depth, currents, and **upwellings.** If great whites are found in tropical areas it is usually in **currents** or upwellings of cold water. They are often found in cool waters in areas with **subtropical** or **temperate** climates.

◄

Most shark species live in or visit tropical waters occasionally.

Migration

Great white sharks often **migrate** as the seasons change, to remain in water of the right temperature. They can swim a long way in a short time. For example, one large great white traveled 118 miles (190 kilometers in two and a half days.

The main reason great whites migrate is to follow their prey. They often target seals, which are a rich food source. The great white shark populations off the Pacific coast of the United States arrive at islands near San Francisco Bay in early April to feed on adult fur seals. Later in April, they migrate south to islands off the coast near Los Angeles, where the seals have their babies. In May, the sharks migrate north to feed on elephant seal babies that were born in the early spring.

Depth

Great white sharks usually live in shallow water. This is because prey is more concentrated here than in the wide, deep ocean. They are found from the surfline to water depths of around 820 feet (250 meters), but usually at around 66 feet (20 meters). Those that live in deeper water move into shallower water to feed. One Australian study discovered that female great whites are more common around islands close to the coast, and males are more common around islands out at sea. This is probably because shallower waters are safer places for females to have their young.

It is very difficult to count wild animals accurately. They may be very small, or spread over a wide area, or look similar. For most animals, their numbers are changing all the time as some die, others are born, and some **migrate** to different areas.

Given their size, great white sharks should be quite easy to count. However, they move fast, live underwater, and inhabit a wide area of the world's oceans. They are not often seen at the surface, so in most cases divers would have to go down to count them. Diving is expensive, and there are obvious dangers from the sharks!

Estimating population

Scientists look at shark populations in two main ways. The first way is called capture-mark-recapture. This method assumes there is an equal chance of catching each individual shark. A number of sharks are caught and a plastic tag attached to them through their **dorsal** fin. Each tag can be individually recognized. The tagged sharks are then released. When any sharks are caught in the future, the number that are tagged is recorded and used to estimate the size of the population.

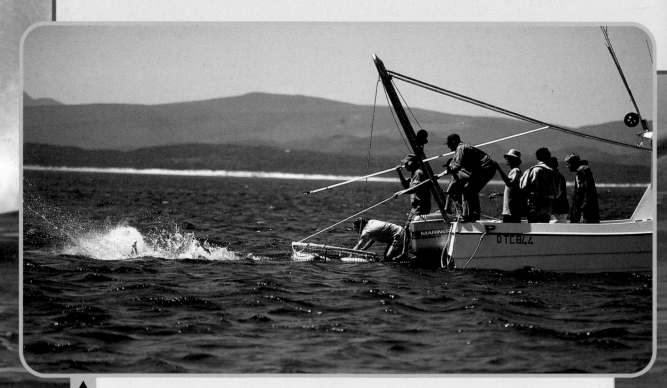

When scientists tag great white sharks, they also record other information such as their size and location. When sharks are later caught, the scientists can see how much they have grown and how far they have traveled.

The number of sharks seen by divers can help estimate the total population size.

There are problems with this method. Catching a great white shark in order to tag it is very difficult because of its size and strength. The tags sometimes fall off, and the capture of a tagged shark may not be reported to the person who tagged it.

A second way of estimating populations is based on the number of sharks caught over time by fishers, or seen over time from boats or by divers. This gives a good idea of whether the population is getting smaller. In the 1960s off southeastern Australia, one great white shark was caught on every 20 shark fishing trips in the same waters. In the 1980s, one was caught on every 650 trips. Great whites are clearly becoming much rarer there. It is now thought there could be as few as 200 great white sharks in southern Australia.

The information that is available suggests that the number of great white sharks is falling worldwide. However, no one knows exactly how many there really are in the world.

Estimating population by tagging

Imagine that 100 sharks are tagged and released. If out of 100 sharks caught later, say that ten have tags. So 10 percent of the sharks caught have tags. It is assumed that the original 100 sharks that were tagged represent 10 percent of the total shark population. In this example, then, the population would be 1,000 because 10 x 10 = 100 percent, and 10 x 100 = 1,000 sharks). This is a simplified explanation. In reality scientists use more complex versions of this method to estimate populations.

The Body of a Great White Shark

Great white sharks are adapted for life in the water. All mackerel sharks have a smooth **streamlined** shape. The body of a great white shark is wide, almost circular in the middle, and tapers at either end to the pointed snout and the tail stalk.

Rough skin

Although a great whites look smooth, its skin feels rough. This is because, like all sharks, it has tiny overlapping **denticles,** or pointed **scales.** Denticles are raised on tiny stalks, unlike the flat scales on a **bony fish.** Each one is shaped to cut through the water. This allows the shark to swim with less effort. Points on the scales also interlock to form tough armor. Very few animals can pierce this protective skin.

Under the skin is a layer of overlapping coils of collagen (strands of protein), somewhat like rubber bands. This smoothes the great white's body. Giant swimming muscles inside a great white's back pull against the backbone and against the tough collagen layer. This produces very powerful swimming strokes for the amount of energy used. A great white uses stiff flicks of its tail **fins** and tail stalk. Keels, or ridges, running along each side of the tail stalk help to strengthen it.

This is a closeup of the denticles on a great white's skin.

Floating and staying level

Great white sharks are heavy animals. A great white is buoyant (able to float) mostly because it has a huge liver full of oil that is lighter than water. However, this alone is not enough to stop the shark from sinking. It also has large **pectoral** fins, that push its body upward with the slightest swimming movement. Although the fins look rigid, great whites move them using muscles to change the angle or speed they swim at.

Breathing under water

All fish breathe using **gills.** These are body parts with thin skin and lots of blood vessels. They transfer some of the oxygen that is dissolved in seawater to blood cells. These transport the oxygen to different parts of the body. They also transfer waste carbon dioxide from the body to the water.

As a great white swims, water is forced into its mouth, across its gills, and out of its **gill slits.** However, it can also breathe for shorter periods by using its throat muscles to pump water into its mouth and across its gills .

You can see this great white's gills in passages behind its throat.

gills

Light skeleton

Sharks are also buoyant because their skeletons are made of **cartilage** and are light. Cartilage is usually flexible, but the cartilage in the parts of a shark that need to be especially strong, such as the jaws and backbone, is rigid and hard.

Staying Active

Great white sharks swim over long distances through the world's cooler oceans to find **prey** that lives there. Most sharks slow down in colder waters, because the low temperature gives them less energy for activity. Great whites and other mackerel sharks, however, can stay active. Although they are **cold-blooded,** they are also warm-bodied.

Warm-bodied not warm-blooded

Warm-blooded animals, such as **mammals,** maintain a constant internal temperature no matter what the temperature of their surroundings. The advantage of this is that their life processes can always happen at the same rate, wherever they are. The disadvantage is that it takes a lot of energy to keep this constant temperature. Warm-blooded animals usually need to eat much more for their size than cold-blooded animals.

Warm-bodied sharks have the advantages of warm-blooded animals without needing to eat as much, although they do eat more than other types of sharks. Great whites can raise their internal temperature up to 55 °F (13 °C) above the water temperature. But this happens only in the parts of their body that are vital for swimming and finding prey. Increased temperatures in the swimming muscles, brain, and intestines make them work more efficiently.

◄

Great white sharks can swim for longer and faster in cold water than most other sharks. They can also spot and catch prey more quickly.

Great white sharks produce a lot of muscle power by reusing the internal heat they make.

Special plumbing

When we run, we create excess heat in our muscles. To avoid overheating, warmed blood moves to the surface near our skin, where it cools as it loses heat into the air. Heat is lost more quickly in cold air than in warm air. As great whites swim in cool water, they could lose heat quickly. However, they have a special circulation system that prevents this from happening. This is a complex network of blood vessels called a *rete mirabile* (pronounced "reet meerahbeelay").

Energy efficiency

A 50 °F (10 °C) rise in a shark's internal temperature can give it three times greater speed and strength and faster digestion of food.

Size for size, great whites need to eat ten times more food than most other sharks.

A meal of 66 pounds (30 kilograms) of whale blubber, or fat, can provide enough energy for a great white shark for six weeks.

In this time, it can swim up to 3,730 miles (6,000 kilometers)!

In the *rete*, hot blood from the shark's swimming muscles moves through small **veins** very close to small **arteries.** These arteries contain oxygen-rich, cold blood from its cold heart and **gills.** Heat transfers from the veins to the arteries, warming up the cold blood. This warmed blood then moves back to the swimming muscles, intestines, and brain. These parts work more efficiently because they operate with prewarmed blood.

Great White Shark Teeth and Jaws

The teeth and jaws of the great white shark are among the most feared in the animal kingdom. This **predator's** success in catching food depends on its teeth being sharp at all times.

A shark may produce tens of thousands of teeth in its lifetime. Each tooth lasts around three months.

Teeth conveyor belt

A great white shark has 100 to 150 teeth at any one time. They are triangular with jagged edges, designed to cut and saw flesh. The teeth nearest the front of the jaw are the biggest. The teeth get gradually smaller towards the corners where the jaws meet. The upper teeth are broader and more curved than the lower teeth. Each tooth is strengthened inside with layers of **minerals.**

Shark teeth are not set firm in sockets in the jaws, like human teeth. Instead they grow from a special membrane. This membrane slowly and continually unfurls from inside the jaw **cartilage,** somewhat like a toothy conveyor belt. The teeth are arranged in two or three parallel rows that follow the line of the jaw. The newest teeth are folded on the inside, the oldest are standing up on the outside. When an old tooth becomes blunt or dislodged as the shark bites, a newer tooth, already formed, moves forward from the row behind to take its place. Each new tooth is slightly bigger than the preceding one, so they grow in size as the shark's body grows.

Loose jaws

As in other sharks, a great white's mouth is under its snout. This might cause a problem when it bites **prey,** because it might have to maneuver its body to bring its mouth forwards. However, great whites have a special adaptation that solves this problem. They have loose, sliding jaws.

As a great white opens its lower jaw to bite, its snout bends upward. Then the upper jaw slides forward and down, along a special groove on the skull. This makes the jaws reach further forward. As the jaws widen, cartilage behind them moves into place to hold them firm, so they can close together without slipping. The jaws clamp teeth into the prey, the snout lowers, and the upper jaw slides back into place. This process is completed within two seconds.

As the shark bites, its eyes roll back into their sockets and this makes the eyes look white. The sockets protect the eyes from damage caused by prey thrashing in the water. Finally, the shark shakes its head from side to side. This causes its upper teeth to cut away the prey's flesh.

A great white's jaws are huge, more than 1 1/2 feet (1/2 meter) wide in the largest individuals. The jaws are made of cartilage, but they can bite with a force of around 3 tons per 0.15 square inch (1 square centimeter).

A Supreme Hunter

Adult great white sharks are **apex predators.** This means they are at the top of the **food chain** and have no natural predators. The only other large predators in the oceans are whales such as **orcas.**

Great white sharks eat a wide range of **prey.** When they are young, they eat mostly small sharks and **bony fish,** such as halibut, but also crabs and squid. As they get bigger they eat larger, faster fish, such as tuna, swordfish, and barracuda, as well as small prey. They also sometimes eat marine turtles, penguins, and starfish.

Saving effort

Sharks, like most predators, prefer to catch an easy meal. Great whites often eat dead whales they are attracted to by the stench of rotting flesh. They also eat fish, such as tuna, caught on **long-lines.** When hunting prey, they often target the weakest or sickest animals in a group, because these are easier to catch.

Fatty food

As they get bigger, great whites also eat marine **mammals** such as sea lions, seals, whales, and dolphins. These animals often take a lot of effort to catch. They are agile, powerful swimmers and often live in big groups so they can warn one another of a shark's approach. However, they are rich in **nutrients** and fat, which are contained in the thick blubber that keeps them warm in cold water. Great whites have large livers and intestines that allow them to digest this fatty food fairly quickly.

Great whites sometimes leap out of the water in pursuit of fast prey such as sea lions.

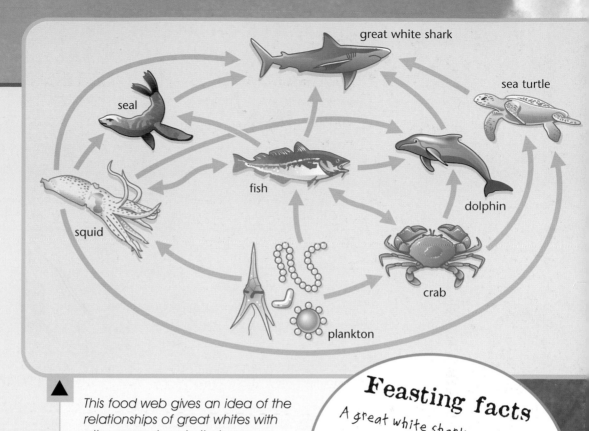

great white shark

sea turtle

seal

fish

dolphin

squid

crab

plankton

▲ *This food web gives an idea of the relationships of great whites with other organisms in their ocean **habitat**.*

Feasting facts

A great white shark can take as much as 51 pounds (23 kilograms) in one bite.

Great whites can attack prey at speeds of up to 31 miles (50 kilometers) per hour.

Getting a meal

Great white sharks usually hunt by ambush. They keep out of sight of their prey by moving through the shadows, close to rocks. They have dark upper sides that cannot easily be seen by prey as they look down toward darker water from above. They also have a white underside that cannot easily be seen by prey from below, looking up into lighter water. This is called countershading.

When a great white has spotted a victim, it swims toward it in a short, high-speed burst. The force of this sometimes knocks the prey clear out of the water. Great whites usually attack from below, but different prey are handled slightly differently. For example, with large elephant seals they attack the head, neck, or rear flippers, and then swim away. Their bite causes a lot of blood loss in the seal. The shark moves in to eat this potentially dangerous prey once it has bled to death. Smaller prey, such as seals, are often caught in the shark's jaws and dragged under water until they drown.

A shark's hunting success improves with experience. In the ocean off California, experienced great whites stay close to colonies of elephant seals at high tide. They know that the beaches where the seals gather get very crowded at high tide, and more seals will enter the water.

Great White Shark Senses

Great white sharks, like other animals, use a range of senses to understand and react to the world around them.

Smell

Sharks can smell amazingly well. They can detect smells as weak as ten drops of blood in a swimming pool. As they swim, water flows into their nostrils where special sacs detect any scents. They are especially sensitive to smells associated with food, such as blood from injured **prey.** Once they have sensed a smell, they swim around until they can locate where it is strongest and then move toward it, usually along ocean **currents.** Sometimes sharks stick their noses out of the water to smell the air and find out where prey are. They might do this to find a colony of sea lions on land.

Sight

Great whites have large eyes that are very sensitive to movement and contrast (light and dark) within a range of 27 feet (25 meters). This is vital in tracking prey or other sharks and in judging their size as they get closer. Shark eyes work ten times better than human eyes in low light conditions. They have a special reflective layer at the back of their eyes called a *tapetum lucidum.* This bounces any available light—even the dim light from stars—toward the most sensitive parts of the eye. When sharks see in daylight, the **iris** closes to protect these sensitive parts.

Unlike any other fish, great white sharks raise their head out of the water to see and smell above the surface.

Bite test

Sharks feel things using their teeth. Shark teeth are full of nerves that can sense hardness. Sensitive pores in their mouth can taste. When great whites approach unfamiliar objects, such as buoys, they often bite them. This is not to cause damage, but to find out what they are.

Hearing and feeling

Sounds travel underwater as vibrations in the water. Sharks detect these vibrations in two ways. They partly use ears inside their skull, that are connected to the outside by two pores, or little holes, behind their eyes. They mainly use their lateral lines, which are a row of pores along each side. Vibrations in the water move fluid trapped behind the pores. Vibrations in the fluid move tiny sensitive hairs. The lateral lines allow a shark to sense vibrations all around its body, not just on its head. Sharks are especially sensitive to the movements of struggling or injured prey.

▲ This great white shark is finding out about an unfamiliar buoy by biting it.

The sixth sense

In addition to sight, smell, hearing, touch, and taste, sharks have a sixth sense, called **electroreception.** All living things produce weak electrical signals. These signals travel well through water. Great whites, like all sharks, have pores dotted over their snout, called **ampullae.** These are full of a jelly-like substance that is attached to nerves that pass information to the brain. The jelly conducts even tiny amounts of electricity in the water to the nerves. Besides detecting electricity caused by prey movements, great whites can also detect Earth's **magnetic field.** So, their ampullae can also help them find their way around as they move through the oceans.

Great white sharks are usually thought of as solitary killers roaming the oceans. In fact, they are much more social animals than we imagine. They may gather in large numbers where there is lots of food.

Dominance

When a number of great whites come together, particularly at feeding sites, there will be some sharks that feed first or that the others stay away from. These are the dominant individuals, the ones the others consider most important. Dominant sharks are usually the biggest and probably the strongest and most dangerous. There are other levels of importance within the group, based on size.

If two great whites approach each other, they turn away at the same time and sometimes swim parallel to each other. Each is seeing how big the other one is, to work out its place in the group.

Avoiding fights

When they are competing for the same **prey,** or at breeding time, great whites feel threatened if others come too close. Their jaws and teeth can kill or seriously injure other great whites that threaten them. However, they rarely fight because they risk being badly injured themselves. Instead, sharks behave in special ways to communicate their feelings.

Great whites interact with other great whites in different, usually peaceful, ways.

A great white shark often slaps the water or other sharks with its strong tail.

Displays

A great white shark that feels threatened **displays** by swimming in an unusually stiff position, with its back hunched and **pectoral fins** held pointing downward. It even does this while swimming upside down. In addition to swimming in a stiff position, the shark opens its nostrils, slides its upper jaw forward, and displays its teeth. This delivers a clear message: "I have sharp teeth I could use on you if I wanted to!" If these displays do not stop another shark, great whites will attack.

They slam their bodies together, or slap each other with their tail fins. These shows of strength usually confirm who is the strongest, and serious fighting is avoided. However, fights with injuries can happen during the breeding season, when rival males may compete for the same female.

Biting

Great whites, especially youngsters, sometimes bump, bite, and then release each other. Just as they test objects and other animals to see if they are good to eat, they test each other to get to know each other. Adult males and females also bite each other when they get close at breeding time. Great whites are protected by their tough **denticles** and rapidly healing skin, but many have scars on their bodies not only from struggling prey, but also from other great whites.

Great White Shark Breeding

We do not know all the details about how great white sharks breed, or produce young. It is thought that they gather together in particular areas of warmer, shallower water to breed. Areas where many baby great whites have been caught by fishers include the Sicilian channel in the Mediterranean Sea (between Sicily and Tunisia) and the Pacific Ocean off southern California.

You can see the claspers on the underside of this male great white.

Mating and eggs

All male sharks mate using two claspers. Claspers are folds of skin with grooves, next to the **pelvic fins.** When two sharks mate, the male often grasps the female's **pectoral** fin to hold her close. His sperm move along the groove of one clasper, inside the female, and fertilize her eggs. (In most other fish, the female's eggs are fertilized outside her body, when the male covers the eggs with his sperm.) Once they have mated, males leave the females.

The fertilized eggs take around a year to fully develop inside a female. There are usually between five and ten fertilized eggs, sometimes more. As the **embryos** develop, they feed at first on the yolk in their eggs. Part of the yolk attaches to their mother's body and taps into her blood. This gives the embryos **nutrients** and oxygen. As the embryos get bigger they also feed on unfertilized eggs, smaller embryos, and their own shed teeth, which provide them with extra **minerals.**

Birth and growth

Like most sharks, great whites give birth to live pups, or babies, instead of laying eggs. The pups hatch out of the eggs inside the mother and are then born. Female great whites give birth to two to ten pups. Newborn pups are about 4 to 5 feet (1.2 to 1.5 meters) long and look just like their parents. They can swim and catch their own food as soon as they are born.

Great white pups grow slowly. They grow more quickly in warmer waters than in cold. Females take 10 to14 years to reach 16 feet (5 meters), the usual size when they become able to breed themselves. Males take 9 to10 years to reach maturity.

Pros and cons of live birth

One of the advantages for sharks of keeping their babies safe inside for longer is that the pups are developed enough to take care of themselves when they are born. This makes them more likely to survive and reproduce themselves in the future. However, as each pup takes up room inside its mother, not many can be produced at one time. Fish that lay lots of small eggs that develop outside their body can have many more young. Another disadvantage is that developing pups use up a female's valuable nutrients, so she has to feed more often while pregnant. A great white female may need a year between giving birth and mating again to build up enough food reserves to be able to have more pups.

▲ *Great white pups are born in spring to late summer, in warm water.*

Young great white sharks face a few **predators** in the wild, including other, larger sharks. For an adult great white, the only natural threat is from a group of hunting **orca** whales. Even so, far fewer great whites are killed by orcas than are killed by people.

People are not much of a match for great white sharks. People are much smaller and weaker and are equipped only with small teeth. People can only take on great whites because they have developed effective weapons and tools and ways of working together. People kill great whites because they think sharks are dangerous and because they can be sold for money. People also kill them by accident, when they fish for other **species,** or when they destroy their **habitats.**

Increasing danger

All sharks are increasingly in danger because of the rapidly rising human population. As more people demand more food, fishing vessels try to catch more fish, including sharks. There are fewer fish to catch, so to make a living the fishers target more valuable species. They do this no matter how rare or **endangered** they may be.

More and more people today live by or visit coasts. This is because of the scenery and weather, the jobs available there, such as fishing and tourism, and because of the lifestyle. Many people visit coasts for watersports, from swimming and boating to diving and surfing.

A person paddling on a surfboard could look like a seal or whale to a great white swimming below.

Shark attack facts

Since 1876, there have been about 370 known attacks on people by great whites, resulting in 69 deaths.

There are around 50 to 75 attacks by different shark species each year, causing 5 to 10 deaths.

People are 30 times more likely to be struck by lightning than to be bitten by a shark.

The number of sharks killed by people each year is between 30 and 100 million.

This man survived being bitten by a great white because it was not really trying to hurt him.

Conflict

The more people there are in the water, the more likely it is that some will come across a great white shark. Great whites will hunt any **prey** they find in the sea, and this sometimes includes people. They have a reputation as regular man-eaters, but although they are one of the most likely shark species to target people, encounters and fatal attacks are surprisingly rare.

It is likely that great whites attack people mostly because of mistaken identity. The most frequent victims are surfers. To a shark swimming below them, a person paddling on a surfboard may look like a small shark, whale, or seal. Great whites test unknown things using their teeth. In most attacks, shark bites injure but do not remove flesh, which sharks easily could if they wanted to. This may be because to a shark, a person does not taste as good as a fat seal or whale!

Shark Fishing

For centuries fishers have tried to catch many kinds of shark, both to eat them and to remove a dangerous creature from the sea. In the last 80 years, they have had a new motive—trophy hunting. Some people like to show off sharks' teeth or the whole jaw, to prove they are expert hunters.

Great white shark jaws are sought-after trophies around the world.

Trophy hunters

Shark trophy hunting became popular in the 1920s in the seas off Australia, South Africa, and the United States. People wanted to show that they could conquer wild beasts on land—such as tigers in Asia—and also catch big fish in the oceans. They tried to catch the biggest, most aggressive fish they could find, including great white sharks. They used strong rods and reels.

In the seas off Australia and South Africa in the 1950s, fishers began to make shark fishing easier. They lured great whites to an area by throwing buckets of fish blood, oil, and guts into the water. This is called **chumming.** The sharks were then hooked at the surface using harpoons, or they were shot from boats. As a souvenir and to prove they had caught a great white, the fishers would have their photos taken back on shore, with the shark strung up on huge scales.

The hunts for great whites increased in the 1980s, following the success of a book and film called *Jaws*. More collectors wanted teeth and well-preserved jaws to show off, without having taken part in the chase. Shark hunters wanted to cash in on this and caught sharks more often using easier methods. For example, they would poison chunks of fish and attach them to thick chains that hung down in the water from empty oil drums. Since the 1990s trade in shark jaws has increased as more people sell and buy over the Internet. A large set of great white shark jaws recently sold for $50,000.

Flesh and fins

People continue to catch and sell sharks to eat. Great white shark meat is eaten fresh, dried, salted, or smoked. Oil is extracted from its liver and sold as a vitamin supplement to fight colds. However, by far the greatest demand is for the **fins** of many sharks, including great whites. Their **cartilage**-rich fins are traditionally used in Asian cooking to make a thick soup.

Shark's fin soup is an expensive luxury. As people in China got richer in the 1980s, even more people could afford shark's fin products. This resulted in more shark fishing all over the world. The majority of sharks caught today are **finned.** This means that their fins are cut off, and their still living bodies are thrown back into the water to die.

▲ Today, fishers sell 2 pounds (1 kilogram) of shark's fin for around $13. In a restaurant, a single bowl of shark's fin soup costs around $120.

The Accidental Killing of Sharks

Trophy hunting for great whites only takes a smal lnumber of great white sharks. The biggest cause of death for sharks of all **species** is **bycatch.** Bycatch happens when fishers catch something accidentally while trying to catch something else. Many **threatened** sea creatures are at risk from bycatch because of the great amount of commercial fishing around the world.

Overfishing

Today, fishing vessels catch so many fish that around 70 percent of all species caught for food are being overfished. This means people are removing far more fish from populations than are being added as a result of breeding. In some areas, once common fish, such as cod and anchovy, are now rare because of overfishing.

Bycatch of sharks happens for different reasons. It is usually because the sharks are hunting the fish that people are trying to catch. Huge ships, sometimes working in pairs, drag extremely long and large nets through the oceans. They catch any fish they can, regardless of their size or rarity. If sharks are caught in nets, they usually drown because water cannot pass over their **gills** fast enough for them to breathe. Other sharks are caught on the numerous baited hooks on **long-lines** attached to tuna ships, or when they eat already hooked tuna.

▶ Sharks, such as great whites, may get caught accidentally on fishing nets and die.

Fishing facts

Of the almost 80 million tons of fish caught each year, nearly 882,000 tons are sharks of all species.

The mouth of one of the world's biggest fishing nets could encircle twelve jumbo jets.

One long-line can carry thousands of baited hooks. Each tuna ship may drop 80 miles (128 kilometers) of line at one time.

A third of all fish caught is ground up into fishmeal. This is used as animal feed or as crop fertilizer.

Around a quarter of all fish caught is unwanted bycatch that is thrown back into the water, dead or alive.

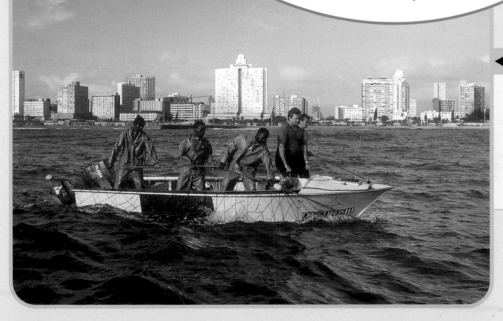

These people are checking a shark net that protects swimmers off the South African coast.

In the past, shark bycatch was usually thrown back into the sea. This was because the price that people could get for sharks was too low to justify the amount of space their bodies would take up on the ships. Now that their **fins** are so valuable, the sharks are usually **finned** before being thrown back.

Shark nets

Sharks are also killed accidentally on shark nets. These strong nets are strung offshore near certain popular beaches and bays to keep people and sharks apart. Sharks, dolphins, and other marine animals often get tangled in them and drown or starve to death.

Destroying Great White Shark Habitats

People are destroying ocean **habitats,** just like they are destroying habitats on land. Underwater, however, a lot of the destruction is hidden from view. When marine habitats are destroyed it affects some **species** more than others. But all are affected because whole **ecosystems** are disturbed. For example, although a **predator,** such as the great white shark, may not be affected directly, it will be affected if there is less **prey** for it to eat.

Destroying the ocean floor

Great white shark populations can suffer badly in areas where the ocean floor is destroyed. Along the coast of California over 80 percent of fish species once thought to be common, including the great white shark, are now considered rare. The great white is among these partly because its favorite prey, such as rockfish, are becoming rare.

The ocean floor is mainly destroyed by a method of fishing that uses bottom trawls. These are wide nets, weighed down with heavy rollers, that are pulled by trawlers across the ocean floor. They are so strong they knock over or sweep up everything they hit. One pass of a bottom trawl can ruin large areas of coastal coral and seagrass that have taken years to establish. These provide shelter and breeding grounds for complex ecosystems of marine creatures such as fish, sea stars, crabs, and sponges. These in turn feed larger fish, sea lions, and **apex predators** such as great white sharks.

▲ *This dead coral was dislodged by bottom trawls. What was once a rich reef habitat is now barren.*

"The way we fish is like hanging a huge net dragged from an airship across a forest, knocking down the trees and scooping up the plants and animals, and then throwing away everything except the deer."
Elliott Norse, biologist

The Mediterranean Sea is highly polluted. This has affected populations of dolphins, monk seals, and many species of fish. Fewer great white sharks are caught by trawlers, partly because pollution has killed their prey and there are not many sharks left in the area.

pollution and development

Some coastal pollution happens as a result of development. For example, governments may encourage tourism in coastal areas because it creates jobs. However, the pollution produced by tourists may ruin local fishing industries.

Pollution

People treat the oceans like a big garbage can. Some of the pollution sinks or breaks up, but most stays around and affects marine life. Most pollution comes from land. Sewage, sludge, oil, fertilizers, and industrial waste are washed off land or dumped into drains and rivers. Other pollution, such as radioactive waste, garbage, and oil washed out of oil tankers, is dumped at sea.

Great white sharks are rarely affected directly by pollution. However, pollutants may affect their prey. For example, fertilizers make marine plants called algae grow so much that they cut out light to the sea floor, killing other algae below. When bacteria break down these algae, they use up so much oxygen in the water that fewer fish can survive there. This means fewer prey for small predators and, through the **food chain,** for sharks.

Dealing with Fishing

The number of great white sharks in places where there used to be many of them has dropped a lot because of the wide range of serious threats they face. Logbooks kept by **long-line** tuna fishing boats, for example, have recorded an 80 percent drop in great white sharks caught as **bycatch** in certain areas. Still, no one knows for sure what the total population once was and what it is now. A drop in one area may simply mean that great whites have moved on and are now abundant in other areas.

However, if great white populations have dropped, they will take a long time to recover. This is because these animals take a long time to grow and mature, and because they have few pups. As a result, several countries have taken steps to protect the remaining great whites around their coasts. These countries took action because people demanded that more should be done to **conserve** great white sharks.

Protecting great whites using laws

The first country to pass laws to protect great white sharks was South Africa. In 1991 it banned the killing, injuring, or sale of great whites or any great white products, such as **fins.** People who break these laws risk heavy fines, having their boat taken away, or even a jail sentence. Nearby Namibia followed South Africa's lead in 1993.

The United States started passing laws to protect great whites in 1994. California passed a bill that prevented commercial great white fishing activities along its coast. Populations of great whites in Atlantic waters off the United States became officially protected in 1997.

▶ *This massive shark was caught illegally in Sicily.*

Today the only legal capture of great whites in California is as bycatch from approved commercial fishing boats and by scientists who have capture permits.

In Australia scientists first proposed in 1995 that **chumming** should not be allowed close to the coast. They also wanted only fishing hooks of smaller sizes. Great whites can only be caught using especially big hooks. They also insisted that shark-cage tourist operators must have a license to run their businesses. The Australian government made this the law in 1997, when the great white shark was officially described as **endangered** and given the protection it needs.

Honesty motivation

Given the protected status of great whites in certain countries, many fishing vessels are reluctant to admit to bycatch. Several governments are offering encouragements, such as money, to fishing vessels who tag and release sharks, rather than kill them or leave them to die. Tags can contain sensitive equipment that records how deep sharks dive and how far they swim, and scientists can track their movements. In this way, conservation scientists can help understand the journeys of great whites through the oceans. Governments can then use this knowledge to improve the protection of great whites.

Illegal chumming was used to entice this great white to take the bait and become hooked.

Saving Great White Shark Ecosystems

The laws made to help **conserve** great white sharks are an important step. However, they only apply to some areas where great whites live. They do not limit **bycatch,** pollution, or fishing practices that destroy marine **habitat.** Still, there are practical ways in which people can help save shark **ecosystems.**

*It takes a lot of time and money to clean up pollution. **Currents** and waves can spread pollution over a wide area. This oil spill was a result of the MV Treasure sinking at Cape Town in 2000.*

Marine reserves

Marine reserves are areas where fishing is banned or closely controlled by wardens, or guards. Access is only allowed if boats or divers have permits. Reserves allow large numbers of fish, including sharks, to gather and breed. It is hoped that their young will restock the adjoining areas. Unlike many land reserves, marine reserves do not have fences around them, so fish and other marine animals come and go. Like any reserves, the larger the area the more expensive it is to keep up. Marine reserves have been set up around Dyer Island off South Africa and the Farallon Islands off California to conserve great white sharks in particular. Many more reserves have been set up around the world to conserve rich ecosystems of marine life, including coral reefs where many different shark **species** live.

Greenpeace, an international conservation group, runs a campaign encouraging countries to protect endangered toothfish, which are victims of pirate fishing.

Changing the fishing industry

It is possible to control fishing to benefit great white sharks, other **threatened** marine creatures, and the people who fish. For example, fishing vessels can reduce bycatch and save marine habitat by not fishing with destructive bottom trawls. Although their catches will be smaller in the short term in the waters around those areas, over a longer period the ecosystem will remain healthy. This means fish can be harvested from the same waters year after year, without their numbers falling.

Many governments make laws to control wasteful bycatch. However, these laws are useless unless they are enforced. To enforce them government observers need to be on board to monitor the number of fish caught and the bycatch. They fine the people who own the boats if catches are more than agreed limits.

Stopping pirate fishing

Pirate fishing is a major problem for governments trying to control fishing in their waters. Governments usually control how much fish a boat from its own country can catch and where it can fish. However, it cannot control boats from other countries. Pirate vessels fish where they please and take as much as they want, including **endangered** and threatened marine animals. They are difficult to stop because they carefully hide their owners' identities by regularly changing names and crews. They always fly flags of convenience. This means they pay money to register with a country that does not enforce fishing restrictions.

Conservation Efforts

Fishing creates jobs for millions of people around the world. Governments are often reluctant to control fishing because it might affect jobs and make the government unpopular. It is also expensive to control fishing, and poorer countries may not have the funds to do it effectively. Governments are more likely to control fishing if members of the public and **conservation** groups encourage them.

Conservation groups

There are many local, national, and international conservation groups dedicated to conserving sharks and marine life in general. Many are nongovernmental organizations (NGOs) such as the World Wildlife Fund (WWF) and Greenpeace. NGOs raise money for conservation from donations by the public and businesses. They raise public awareness of the dangers to all sharks, using advertising campaigns and fundraising events. They also sometimes take more direct action, such as revealing the identities of pirate fishing boat owners or preventing shark killing.

Specialist shark scientists employed by NGOs often advise governments on how best to improve conservation. The World Conservation Union (IUCN) is an international group that has a Shark Specialist Group. It combines government and NGO science experts. The Group makes recommendations to governments around the world on how best to control shark fishing and where to create **marine reserves.** It also campaigns with other groups to make **finning** illegal.

Undercover conservation workers discovered this shop in Hong Kong full of shark fins. Most of them came from illegal finning.

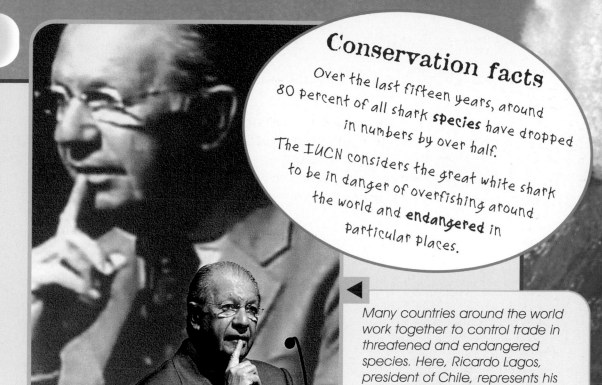

Many countries around the world work together to control trade in threatened and endangered species. Here, Ricardo Lagos, president of Chile, represents his country in the 12th CITES Convention in 2002.

Acting internationally

Great white sharks travel long distances. This means that although local conservation laws are important, they can only be effective if they extend into national and international waters. For example, great whites are partly protected in the important breeding area of the Sicilian Channel in the Mediterranean Sea. However, once they enter the waters near the country of Tunisia, they are unprotected.

Trade in shark trophies and **fins** between countries is controlled and regulated by the Convention on International Trade in Endangered Species of Wild Fauna and Flora (CITES, pronounced "sightease"). CITES works in cooperation with law enforcement people around the world to prevent the illegal smuggling of shark parts.

Consumer power

Large-scale shark killing will continue as long as people want to buy shark meat and fins, jaws and teeth. WWF has helped set up the Marine Stewardship Council. This group encourages shoppers to only buy legally caught fish and fish products that are labeled. An example of this approach is the labeling of dolphin-friendly tuna. Although the **long-lines** catch fewer dolphins than the large nets of the past, they still catch many sharks.

Great White Shark Tourism

Coming face to face with a great white shark is many people's worst nightmare. However, a surprising number of people are happy to pay for the chance to get up close. There are advantages and disadvantages for great whites in these meetings.

Getting too chummy

In the early days of tourist cage diving in Australia in the 1980s, tourist companies offered pay-for-view trips. If no shark showed up, the companies did not get paid. So, many companies started to chum. Excessive chumming, as happened off the coast of California in the 1990s, attracted lots of sharks. But it also increased shark attacks on local surfers and divers because the sharks learned to associate people with food. Another result of this association is that great whites in certain areas will approach boats. Shark hunters in boats can then easily kill them.

Getting closer

Tourists get close to great whites by taking boat trips to known shark locations, such as Dyer Island off South Africa and Dangerous Reef in Australia. Some tourists watch sharks when they rise to the surface to feed. Others in wetsuits and **scuba** gear are lowered under the waves in large, reinforced cages. The sharks approach cages and boats out of curiosity, but also because people lure them to the area by **chumming.**

Steel shark cages float at the surface. The divers inside are closely examined by the sharks.

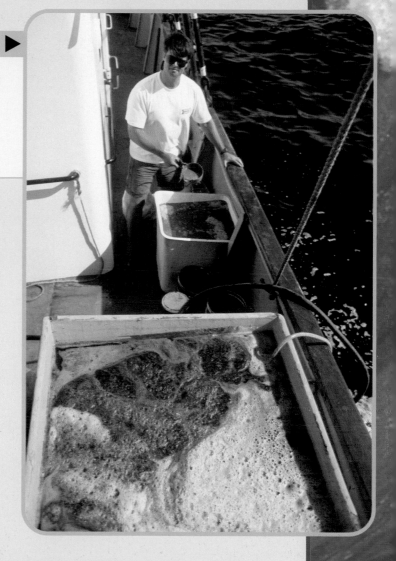

Shark tourist boats should use enough chum to attract great whites, but not feed them, because this may encourage attacks on people.

Helpful tourism

Shark tourism can have positive effects. Some money from shark tourism, including visitors' tickets, cage permits, and items such as posters and T-shirts, goes directly to **marine reserves** and **conservation** groups. Some goes to private tourist boat operators. Visitors also learn more about great whites and are more likely to support shark conservation in the future.

Several conservation groups run their own shark tourism ventures. South Africa's White Shark Research Institute does this. Tourists pay or volunteer to become shark scientists for a while. They may photograph and film sharks to recognize individuals by markings and **fin** shape, and make observations about their behavior.

The other side of tourism

Any kind of tourism in which people see protected animals in the wild raises a difficult question. How do you let enough people get close in order to make money without affecting the animals and their **ecosystem?** More tourists in an area may mean more litter, garbage, and other pollution. Noise from lots of boats and cages may disturb other animals such as fur seals, whales, and seabirds.

The Future for Great White Sharks

By 2003 great white sharks were legally protected in only a few countries. Their long-term survival can only be achieved by international laws, that are enforced by countries all over the world.

CITES listing

The Australian government, backed by a variety of **conservation** groups, is trying to get the great white shark listed by CITES. CITES keep two lists of **threatened** and **endangered** animals. Those in Appendix I risk **extinction** without lots of protection, and those in Appendix II need to be closely monitored because they are threatened. CITES listing for great whites has been slow to come since it was first suggested in 1998. This is because although reductions in great white **bycatch** suggest falling populations, actual population sizes are not known. It is not certain whether the great white shark is rare or not, but listing would create a reason for shark protection worldwide.

Recent advances in great white shark study

People who study great whites learn new things about them every year. Here are just two recent findings:

· *Regional variation*
In different places great whites look different. California sharks have dark gray backs and thin bodies. South African sharks have fawn or olive backs and fatter bodies. This suggests there are distinct populations in the Atlantic and Pacific Oceans.

· *Electrical defence*
In the future, people, such as divers and surfers, who spend time in waters with great white sharks will be able to repel, or drive away them away. Protective Oceanic Devices, or PODs, create an electrical field that irritates the **ampullae** on a shark's snout, making it swim away. These devices can also be put on offshore shark nets and fishers' **long-lines** to protect the sharks.

The future for great white sharks is extremely uncertain.

Knowing more

We know little about many aspects of the great white shark's life. Many more years of observation and monitoring by scientists are needed to better understand them. We know they are slow to grow and reproduce, so they will always be in danger of threats from people. It is important to find out where exactly in the world's oceans they breed. Then we will know which areas we must protect.

What we do know is that great whites are being killed in great numbers. If we do not protect them now, these awesome animals may well be lost to future generations.

Breeding sharks in captivity?

When wild populations of some **species** are low, captive breeding programs in sanctuaries can restock the wild. This has proved successful for animals such as American alligators. However, great white sharks have never survived long in captivity and do not breed there. There are several problems. Great whites are wide-ranging **predators** that need a lot of food and space to survive. They do not get this in captivity. Also, the weak electrical fields created by equipment in aquariums can disturb great whites' **electroreception,** severely affecting how they sense their surroundings. Breeding in captivity will only become possible if people can learn more about these creatures.

It may be difficult to imagine how you can help great white sharks, but there are some simple things you can do to make a difference to their lives. The important thing to remember is that the people who make laws around the world protecting sharks listen to the opinions of people just like you.

Learn about shark conservation

The more you know about the problems facing sharks, the more effectively you can join in helping them. Read books, watch documentaries, or visit some of the many websites devoted to sharks. You may be lucky enough to visit a local museum, zoo, or aquarium with a shark exhibit, or even go on a shark-watching trip. Once you know more about the practice of **finning,** for example, you can tell your friends and family. You could even suggest sharks as a school study topic.

Get writing

You need to tell decision makers how you feel about the numbers of sharks being killed. There are several good ways to do this. You can add your signature to an existing petition (a letter whose thoughts you agree with) started by a **conservation** group. In 2000 the U.S. government was debating whether to ban finning in U.S. waters. WWF organized 18,000 messages in support of the Shark Finning Prohibition Act. These messages encouraged the Act to be made law.

Although aquariums will not have live great white sharks, they are good places to learn more about all types of shark. This is a model of a great white shark recently displayed in an aquarium.

Know your subject by reading as much as you can about sharks.

Write your own letters demanding a change in the way great white sharks are treated. Many shark conservation groups can provide help with wording a letter so it has the greatest effect. Letters like this can then be used in a variety of ways. You could start your own petition and ask local stores, schools, and libraries for space to leave it for others to sign. You could send a letter directly to your state representatives. You could write to your newspapers.

Buy carefully

The shark killing industry is encouraged by demand. Encourage others to avoid all shark products. For example, do not eat at restaurants that serve shark's **fin** soup, and tell them why you will not. Never buy shark trophies such as teeth and jawbones.

Donate

Most people do not have a lot of money to donate to shark conservation groups. Encourage people to give as much as they can. You can do this by taking part in a sponsored activity or by joining with others to sponsor a shark. You could volunteer your time with shark campaigners in your local town or city. If you do this and you have learned a lot about sharks, you will also be able to answer people's questions.

Glossary

ampullae   jelly-filled pits sensitive to electricity

apex predator   animal that eats other animals and is so big or strong that usually no other animals kill or eat it

artery   blood vessel that transports blood cells carrying oxygen

bony fish   fish that have skeletons made of hard bone

bycatch   what is caught accidentally when trying to catch fish

cartilage   tough but flexible tissue containing collagen, such as that found in human ears or shark skeletons

cartilaginous fish   fish, such as sharks, with cartilage skeletons

chumming   throwing things such as dead fish and blood into the sea to attract other fish, such as sharks

climate   general weather pattern

cold-blooded   animal whose body temperature changes with that of its surroundings

conservation   protecting wildlife and the natural habitats of the world

current   stream of water in an ocean moving in a particular direction, often with a different temperature to the stiller water around it

denticles   shaped sharp scales

display   special behavior, often using particular body parts or positions, with a particular meaning

dorsal   attached to or part of the back

ecosystem   community of animals and plants that interact or affect each other's lives in a particular area

electroreception   an electrical sense

embryo   unborn or unhatched offspring

endangered   so few in number that the animal or plant may not survive much longer on Earth

extinct   no longer living on Earth

fin   flap of skin, with or without bones inside, used for swimming

finning   cutting off and keeping fins and throwing the remains of the body back into the sea

food chain   shows the order in which food energy passes from plants to animals

gills special body parts found in all fish, used to breathe underwater

gill slits slits on cartilaginous fish where water leaves the body after passing over gills

habitat place in the natural world where a particular organism lives

iris part of eye that changes shape to control how much light enters

long-line long fishing line with many hooks attached

magnetic field pattern of magnetic force around Earth. Many animals use it to find their way around.

mammal warm-blooded animal with hair and a backbone that can feed its young with milk from its body

marine reserve area where fishing is banned or closely controlled

migrate move from one place to another, often because it offers better feeding or climate

mineral chemical, such as calcium, needed by living things

nutrients chemicals that plants and animals need in order to live

orca large black and white toothed whale

pectoral attached to or part of the chest

pelvic attached to or part of the pelvis (hip area)

predator animal that hunts, kills, and eats other animals

prey animal that is hunted and eaten by another animal

scale thickened piece of dead surface skin

scuba underwater breathing equipment of air tank and mouthpiece

species group of living things that are similar and can reproduce together to produce healthy offspring

streamlined shaped to move smoothly through water or air

temperate describes areas with warm summers and cold winters

threatened at risk of becoming endangered

tropical warm areas of Earth north and south of the equator

upwelling upward movement of colder water from the seafloor

vein blood vessel that transports blood cells carrying carbon dioxide

vertebrate animal with a backbone

Websites

Wildaid
www.wildaid.org
A site presenting a variety of **conservation** initiatives. In 2003, there was an e-petition on WildAid's website calling for shark **finning** to be banned around the world.

National Coalition for Marine Conservation
www.savethefish.org
The website of the U.S. National Coalition for Marine Conservation, which works to conserve fish by preventing overfishing, reducing **bycatch,** and protecting **habitat.**

WWF
www.panda.org
WWF is a large global organization committed to protecting the natural world. Their site contains lots of information about their conservation work for sharks and many other animals.

Greenpeace
www.greenpeace.org
Greenpeace actively campaigns to save marine **ecosystems** from overfishing, pollution, and other threats.

Other shark conservation websites

www.flmnh.ufl.edu/fish/organizations/ssg/ssg.htm
IUCN has a Shark Specialist Group, a group of specialist shark scientists who advise governments and conservation groups about shark biology and populations.

www.flmnh.ufl.edu/fish/sharks/isaf/isaf.htm
This University of Florida site is full of good material on shark attacks, among other things.

Books

Baldwin, Carol. *Sharks*. Chicago: Heinemann Library, 2003.

Deady, Kathleen W. *Great White Sharks*. Mankato, Minn.: Capstone Press, 2001.

Murray, Julie. *Great White Sharks*. Edina, Minn.: Abdo & Daughters, 2002.

Westwood, Brett and Mark Carwardine. *Great White Shark: Habitats, Life Cycles, Food Chains, Threats*. Austin, Tex.: Raintree/Steck Vaughn, 2000.

Index